Love and Cheese
Expressions of Love

By Shannon McEwen

Filidh Publishing

Contents

Love and Cheese – Shannon McEwen

Love and Cheese – Shannon McEwen

Love and Cheese – Shannon McEwen

Love and Cheese – Shannon McEwen

Forward

There are so many expressions of love, from the love of self, of a child, of a mother, of a higher purpose, of a friend or lover. Love is the fabric of our life, knitted into every fibre of our beings. Out of all the emotions I have felt love is what has kept me going, driven me to be who I am and continues to be the force that motivates me. Love has carried me through moments where nothing else could have.

Love is sometimes everlasting and sometimes shorter lived, but regardless of the duration, at its peak it can shine so brightly, the grayest of days seem like sunny August afternoons. Love is sometimes as effortless and innate as breathing, but it isn't always as easy as modern fairy tales would have us believe. It's work, just like any other endeavour that is worthwhile. Love is a great foundation to anything, where we build upon, grow from, learn from and move forward from.   It's sweet, messy, funny, romantic and life changing.

So, with this, I share the moments I have felt love, breathed it, lived it, moved forward or stood still because of it. I encourage you to follow along on my journey, feel what I have felt, cry when I have cried, laugh when I have laughed and most importantly love, like I have loved. My words are as always, an infinitesimal piece of my soul, that I place with you, to hold for just a moment. May my words linger long after you have finished this book.

Love, must always, start with self, otherwise we cannot truly understand it.

>Into storms
>Vines entangled
>Protect me
>
>Select me
>For survival
>All because
>
>We love
>In tears
>Laughter
>Even fears
>
>And because
>Of love
>I remain

Dedication

To Dustin, who I believe was a gift from God, to teach me, that I am worthy of love, without the need to do anything but love in return. You are my oasis in the epicentre of chaos, even when I myself am the creator of the chaos.

Acknowledgements

Thank you to Zoe Duff, my publisher, who works tirelessly for Canadian authors, with passion and commitment. I appreciate you.

Silvina Lanusse, who is not only the artist for my cover, but someone I admire greatly.

Tracey Carlson, who continues to be my number one fan. We all need someone like you, I am just lucky to have YOU.

To my darling babies, my family and friends; my reasons for moving forward. For always being my sounding board, my inspiration and my editors, critics and biggest fans.

Thank you, Tal Ball, for all the help with the cover art, for your continued friendship and support.

Love and Cheese – Shannon McEwen

Part I: Unconditional Love, the Love of a Mother

I have been a mother for nineteen amazing, kamikaze plunging, gut-wrenching, thrill riding years and I can safely say it ain't easy, but without a doubt it's worth every moment.

A reason to get through the day

A three-car accident
Before the abandoned vehicle
On the Ironworker's bridge

And a speed trap
Through rush hour

After a hectic day
Interviews and reviews
Politics and policies

And a quick three o'clock
Nibble
Of a wilted sandwich

A brief moment
Of silence
Before being swept
Into a whirlwind

Of chatter
And bickering
With yet more
Daycare overtime

It's a quarter to seven
With tomorrow
Sure to be a repeat

And from the backseat
"Mama, I'm gonna keep you"
With a chubby grin
In the rear view

Love and Cheese – Shannon McEwen

Ain't nothing like it

Squishy hugs with chubby arms
Long fingers clasped
Around dark strands of hair

Cherub face pressed
Against a weary shoulder

Before rising
Puckered lips
Encircling sticky cheeks

Nine and one-half smooches
Before my heart
Melts

Like chocolate
When lips part

To utter
"la u"

Almost a gentleman

Chipmunk voice
From other side
Of green van door

Sweeps smile
So many miles
From tip
Of pink tongue

To stretch lips
Slip swiftly
To pull corners
Of tired eyes

"I wanna open
The door for you
Mama"

"But don't wanna
Get my hands wet"

As big green eyes
Peer back
Into mine
In instant love

Clarity

In the early light of day
I sit and ponder love
And all it has to say

Between it and me
I can plainly see
That it
Pulls me through

You
  And you
    And you too

That's all that counts
When fear mounts
Where worry piles
Carries me these miles

Through darkness
In the brilliant light
Gives me better sight
And dear knowledge
I simply
Must hold on tight

Complete in his trust

In the darkened house
A quarter past ten
Before the house settles in

She carries all fifty pounds
Of warm sleepy boy
To the potty

A drowsy voice
"I hate this"
Before a gruff response
"I know buddy"

His head bobs gently
Against a strong shoulder
As chocolate eyes slip closed

Early morning conversations

Warmth in the semi darkness
Before the crow of the cock
Certainly well before
The horrible squall
Of a very insistent alarm clock

Snuggled close, hand on cheek
He opens his chipmunk voice
And softly speaks
"Mama, what kinds of bears are there?"

To which my eyes sleepily open
My heart beats in pride
Cracked lips lift and spread
Open to wisely confide
As Love wells ever so bright

An instant feeling of right
An unexpected reply
"Teddy bears, cartoon bears, gummy bears, pooh bears"
And a munchkin sigh

Before a pause
As the chipmunk gathers thought
"I meant real bears
Like brown bears, and black bears and polar bears"

A sigh of my own
"Oh yeah, those bears too"
And then the most beautiful sound
Right to the very centre of my soul rebounds

A giggle, followed by a wiggle
To get just a little bit closer
Not realizing
He's at the very middle - of my beating heart

Four-year-old wisdom

Through the confusing haze
Of snot and pain
And over the counter pain killers
His voice whispers
Cracks a little from the newness
Of keeping quiet

As he rubs my back
With a chubby little hand
"it's all right mamma, don't cry
It's gonna be okay"

He pauses in his words
Pats my head
Which ricochets fresh pain
Across the back of my head
And spikes through
My red eyes

And through the agony
I hear him again
"Wanna paint?"

Love and Cheese – Shannon McEwen

From the mouths of babes

A little hand reaches
Wipes away the tears
A little voice teaches
To take away the fears
Somewhere in the
Darkest reaches of night
He shines his innocent light
With confidence states

"My sister says love
Gets rid of monsters

She gives me kisses
And little wishes
But they fade away
So I'm just gonna snuggle
If that's ok"
Then he reached around
With his little arm
Held me close
Far away from harm
And didn't you know
It worked.
Like a charm

Lessons in love

What could I teach you
That you don't already know
You're the kinda kid
That goes against the flow

Nothing and nobody
Can move you somewhere
You don't wanna go

So I'm not sure
What I can show
Except this profound love

That starts in my soul
And explodes
In brilliant shades
To my baby toes

And ain't nothin'
That's gonna ever
Make that love fade

So I guess it's all I got
And all I am
This love
That breathes repeatedly
In and then out

Finnegan

dirty feet
and freckled noses
sand castles
scattered buckets
where littered
shovels
And wet towels
show happy days
Swimming like fishes
along the shore
Between flips
And floating along
Under the sun
campfires
where marshmallows
catch fire and end
in sticky faced
smiles

Love can stink

A pile of feet
Lead to smiling faces
Pressed together
Eyes laughing downward
To the newest addition

A perfect moment
Broken by one cacophonous echo
Against faux suede cushions
Lingering aroma mingles with giggles
As feet hit the carpet and scatter

Love and Cheese – Shannon McEwen

Love is

Three in the morning a babe cries
Exhaustion overwhelms, the noise increases
No choice, she peels her body from the sheet
To tend her little man

Six O'clock, the sun is waking
Another's cry, weak but urgent
As vomit fills the hall, hits the walls
On her hands and knees, she wipes away
The filth, her other hand extends in comfort

The clock strikes twelve, life is hectic
The laundry monster grows
Alphagetti scatter with giggles
Grape juice stains white cotton
Like blood seeps from a wound

The bewitching hour arrives
Among books, chatter,
Bubbles splash across tiles
The growl of her stomach
Surrounded by love she forgot to eat

Love's reflections

In quiet of morning
The solitary sound
Of the bedroom fan

Back and forth
Swish, swish, swoosh

As I sit on the bed
In the faint light
Of early peaking sun

Before I wander
Room to room
To gaze at them

Peacefully asleep
Blissfully unaware
And unburdened

My overtaxed mind
Takes solace
In loves reflections

Made with love

Chocolate chips
Creamed
Into brown sugar
Permeate the air
Mingled giggles
And messed up hair

Growing night
By kitchen light
Atmosphere filled
With care

Along with cookies
Slowly, wholly
Taking shape
Mixed between
Crumbly smiles

Well spent miles
Of nothing
But my love
Mixed
Into the bowl

Midnight revelations of real love

In the latest hour of the night
I sit
And watch you sleep

Stroke your chubby cheek
No silly grin
Or cranky pout

Just the innocence
Along with the occasional sigh

And ten little piggies
Peaking out from under
Your favourite blanket

And in this exact moment
I understand life

Love and Cheese – Shannon McEwen

Mother's Day card

His sincerest words
Trying so very hard
In the homemade card
He poured his love

Where it slowly seeps
To the very marrow
Where old fears I keep
Begin to gently heal

Mingled with salty drops
Splashed silently down
Blue construction paper
Transforms this worried frown

Soaking into the words
An effort to feel
This child's incredible love
So beautifully real

My heart in his
And his hand in mine
Suddenly, inexplicably
Everything's just fine

This very simple moment
With such love to hold me
Until it's all I can see
In a very complex time

In her eyes

In her eyes
I see all things
I could have done better
And all the things
I did just right

In her eyes
I see all the life
I could have missed
And all the light
When she hugs
Me tight

In her eyes
I see all the pain
She soaks in
I know it's mine
But she's the one
Who fights

In her eyes
I see all the love
And I learn so much
More than she did

In her eyes
I see her mother
And am surprised
How I look
In her eyes

Precious

Chubby fingers encased in slim ones
A pull, a twist, a contagious giggle
Two humongous brown eyes
Almost hidden by a life size grin
He stares up with a mischievous twinkle
Before he escapes and rushes off
Energy defined in every movement
As he screams out "COOL CAR"
A Hot Wheel in one hand, a Tonka in the other
Two years ago today marks the beginning
Of a beautiful love, my little man

The crack of early

There was a wiggler
A terrible giggler
Trapped in my bed

Wanting to be fed
With kisses and hugs
Strange little thug

Couldn't tell time
Or understand
Sleep is sublime

His particular brand
Of morning affection
Should be banned

A heady confection
Wrapped in love
And sunbeams above

Right to my tired heart
I'll grudgingly admit
My frown came apart

Love and Cheese – Shannon McEwen

The poetry of love

Finnegan poops in mustardy stanzas
    Always in messy threes
        When I asked him about line breaks
    He pooped upon my knees

Meghan burps her ABC's
    And giggles when she's done
        Then she sings in single syllables
    Thick with witty pun

Logan whines in flawless rhythm
    As he walks in perfect time
        Of every emotional melody
    And the odd poetic rhyme

Daddy laughs in silly sonnets
    And tells jokes in metered verse
        He forgets to pick up the milk
    His memory be his curse

Mama likes us all in line
    From the tallest to the small
        Silent, safe and all tucked in
    Is her most desired poetry of all

Therapy

We walked today
Just her and I
She met my pace
I stared at her beautiful face

And at her crooked smile
She said she hates
Pink curls bouncing
With the shrug
Of her shoulders

Slowly we travelled
And I marveled
At the love I feel
For this every growing
Beautiful girl

So much sparkles
In those hazel eyes
As she talks about
The things she loves

And when she looks at me
And those eyes say
She loves me too
I want to cry

Because I'm the luckiest
The one she calls mom

When she rushes forward
For a hug
That either I need
Or she does
Or as things happen
We both do

My first true love
And she has no idea
Just how amazing
Every part of her is

Mahalo

Afternoon sun
Soaks into parched skin
I sit
For moments
Reflection
Introspection

To clear minds chaos
And focus
On Gods paradise
Here on earth

Clear blue skies
Happy cries
When a boy catches
Then releases
His first fish

Music in the air
Laughter
Carried on
Warm breezes
To everywhere

And for a moment
I can forget
All worries
And cares
And just be one
With all creation

Super heroes

Sticky fingers
And chocolate faces

Giggling grins
And running limbs

To see the winners
Of water park races

Sunshine kisses
On freckled noses

Innocent wishes
And silly poses

Capes that flutter
In the breeze

And through his eyes
For a minute
I can see

What it's like
To just be

Love and Cheese – Shannon McEwen

Little invaders

Honey hair
tangled
Across the pillow case

Tummy pressed
Into the mattress
Bum
Slightly in the air
Without nary a care

Pink striped
footy Jammies
In size six
Diagonally
Splayed across
The bed

Who knew
Such a little
girl

Could
take up such
A big space
In my heart

A Mama's grace

When she was lying there
In that bed
Part girl - Part machine
Blood and fluid
Drip, drip, dripping Into her
Nothing I could do
But watch
Hold the palest hand I'd ever held
So instead we laughed
At the soup -- And the doc
Who looked like
A backstreet boy
And every now
And again
I'd turn around
To wipe away
The tears and the buckets of snot
Before I turned back
To smile at the girl
Who stole my breath
And now that her cyborg
Days are gone
We still laugh at soup
And she still steals my breath
And every moment
I remember
Just how close I came
To losing my grip
On those pale beautiful fingers
And I raise my wet face
To whatever God that'll listen
With thanks

Exponential expectations

Even though
I always knew
I really wanted to
Meet it all
Kissing cheeks
And juggling balls
Minutes
Turned to miles
Changed
To weeks
Writing a list
That never seemed
To end
For them
And him
And her too
Worrying
In darkness
Rushing in blue
Every best intention
Mixed
With hopeful wishes
And the dishes
Piled
Precariously high
So subtly
Hiding
This ragged sigh
And these two
Silent tears
I cry

The answer to why

What's after
A million and nine?
Why the rest
Of the reasons
I love you
Baby mine
Why is the sky blue?
Because
It shines like
The colour
Of your eyes
To remind me of you
Why did the bad guy
Do that?
So that we could
Snuggle
Just a little longer
All safe and snug
Me and my
little love bug
All of your questions
And all of your tries
Make the love
Shine more and more
out of my eyes
So keep asking your questions
And I'll keep loving
You more
With every
One of your "why's "

The smell of love

With the first red leaf
Nostalgia hits
And lips lift

The scent of
new paper
and fun of new
supplies

Back to routines
Haircuts
school fees
And chaos

And the odd
feeling of love
of the 8 am call

"Mom, Finnegan
won't leave the house"

And the cranky
chipmunk voice
as I not so gently
Coax his butt out the door

And my favourite,
the two muttered
"I love you Mama"
before the click on
the other end

Motherhood

I came with no degrees
Or doctorates
Diplomas
Previous experience

Not even particularly
Good
Educated guesses

Did a lot
What not to do's
Did none of the
Crying it outs

Took less than a fraction
Of advice
Of well meaning
Masses

Oh but the love
From their eyes
That match mine

Makes me hope
Perhaps
I've mastered
A thing or two

Love and Cheese – Shannon McEwen

Grade One

Stunning hazel eyes blink in a sleepy haze
From the comfort of tangled blankets
A little brunette's face lights up at the mention
She is now a big girl, no more half days
School supplies placed in her "Bratz" backpack
A new outfit for her grand entrance
A bundle of nerves – she reassures me
My six-year-old angel in Kim Possible gear
She is ready for the world
Armed with Crayola and glue sticks
Secure in the knowledge that she is gorgeous

Five-and-a-half-year-old wisdom

A tone only a boy of five can master
Reverent and arrogant both
With wide eyes
Lips lifted up; enamel twinkles

Honest brown orbs meet weary green
Matter of fact declaration
"I'm not gonna tell you your belly's big and fat
 even if it is"

"Cause that's not nice"
A reassuring pat
Followed by a proud swagger
He skips away; vindicated

Love and Cheese – Shannon McEwen

How to tell she's extraordinary

A quarter abandoned
On the dirty grocery floor
She Smiles, bends

And grasps her bounty
Tightly
In a nine-year-old fist

Rushes up the aisle
Skirts the gumball machine
A predetermined path

To Customer Service
Where she slips the silver
Into the donation box

Take-off

Green eyes light up
Stare out
Through dirty
Airplane pane
Fingers pressed against
The sides
Unable to hide
The smiles
Seatbelt barely able
To contain boy
Lips lifted so high
Made me want
To cry
Happy, happy tears
Of joy
To see that face
All lit up again
So these same green eyes
Pressed up next
To his
And watch us
Take off
Then laugh
When he turns a little
The colour
Of those beautiful eyes
Before these giggles
Turn to sighs
As I lean back
And close my lids
For a moment
Just thank God
For the precious gift
Of this kid

Part II: Love of Self

Before you can love another well, it's always best to learn to love oneself. This can be the hardest journey of them all.

Clean slates

This new day dawns
Fresh page
Full of three hundred sixty-five
Pristine blank pages
Eager to be filled
With adventure
Of my own choosing
No disguise
Or subterfuge
A path forward or frozen in time
Truth here in daylight
Or the same
Comfortable old lies
So here I walk
On my new path
Of complete truths
Shed the mantle
Of my youth in freedom
And trust
in a higher power
I walk with you without fear
So near the light
Not afraid
Of the darkness
In the night
Despite
These insecurities
That bite
At my heels
I'm standing strong
In faith
Full of love
And I long
To fill these pages
Full of bright

What do you see?

In your eyes
What do you see
When you look at me?
Is it the green
That are my eyes
Or the insecurity
Of what lies deep beneath
Buried in my sighs
Or the pain even
Deeper seated inside
My soul
Where the little girl
Is curled up
In the darkest corner
Or is it the tears
That drip down
This face
When I see the worlds
Between the beauty
And the broken
And the words left unspoken
Written all over
Their beautiful souls
Shattered
Waiting to be made whole
Once more
Or is it just the woman
Standing here
Trying to be brave
In the face of it all
Holding up these
Tired bones
Wishing wishes
Not of riches
But simply asking
Not to fall

Gates to heaven

I will enter your door
With dirty feet
Bare from walking
Mouth chapped from talking

Halo bent
And tarnished
Crooked
And askew
Green eyes twinkling

From the joy
I've found in serving
Those who needed me

In my feeble attempts
To be the love
I imagine Jesus
To be

And I will fall
At your beautiful feet
And ask for your grace
All the same

Without guilt
Or shame
Or a modicum of blame

Just my freckled face
Lifted to you
In the utter childlike faith
Of my humanity

Rainy cafes

In this cafe
Steam from my mug
Of English breakfast
Here at my elbow

At the window
Rain all around me
Falls with the
Contemplation inside
My head

Like Mother Nature's
Mixed up
With my creativity
Coming out to be fed

Blending brains
And rains
In some oddly
Beautiful melodic
Refrains

And I tap my fingers
Softly on the tabletop
Next to my tea

Humming and thinking
Just a little
Off-key

Glad for a moment
For the cafe
And the rain
And the solace
Of silence
And me

Room without doors

She sat there
For so long
In the corner
Of this old room

The five-year-old girl
Green eyes
Staring soulfully
Up through dark hair

Fair skin face
Covered
In dirty
Tear stained tracks

Never aging
  Never raging
    Never lying
But sadly crying
Always speaking truth
In the broken innocence
Of her youth

Wondering now
H1ow you made it through
Into this room
Without a door

Where she's been here
All this time
Inside my mind
Way too honest
To be kind

Never aging
  Never raging

Love and Cheese – Shannon McEwen

Never lying
But sadly crying
Always speaking truth
In the broken innocence
Of her youth

While outside the weather
Changing
The emotions ranging
All the topics constantly
Rearranging

What I know to be true
She simply sat
Pushed up against
The wall
Knees against her chest

Hugging the only one
She could attest
Would keep her trust
Which cruelly
Was herself

But not without
Hope mixed the call

Yet you walked in
As if no walls at all
As if No years had past
As if No tears had fallen

Let the sunshine in
To this darkened room
Warmth soak in
To the dampened gloom
Where she sat

Never aging
  Never raging
    Never lying
But sadly crying
Always speaking truth
In the broken innocence
Of her youth

Now my biggest question
Of all remains

Will she escape
Into the light
Will she Let you help me
Set it right?

Or will she remain
Sitting in the corner
Of that room
In the gloom?

Singing off key
Lullabies
To help the time go by

For now she sits just
Inside the safety of her room
In your arms
Holding tightly on
Looking into the brilliant
Blueness of the sea

Liking the smell
And freshness of the trees
As only a child can

Love and Cheese – Shannon McEwen

Not worrying
About what will be

Never aging
  Never raging
    Never lying
But sadly crying
Always speaking truth
In the broken innocence
Of her youth

Born to stand out

For a moment
No barriers
Just the truth

Brilliant beautiful light
Before the door
Is gently closed
Behind us

And the librarian
Sternly points
To the sign on the wall

And the coldness
Of tears sting my eyes
As I try to remember
The moment

Where the fears
Didn't rule
My actions

And the rulers
Didn't divide
Me into factions

I could just open
These green eyes
Let out these sighs

Sit in the warmth
Of your sun
In beautiful salvation

Freedom from guilt
Shame
Constant blame

Somehow knowing
I am loved
Without the words
Having to be said

Love and Cheese – Shannon McEwen

Bobcat

I stood here
you stood
There

From across
The grass
We locked gazes

Big fat
Salted drops
Dripped

Slipped
From the corner
Of green eyes

Down freckled
Cheeks
For what
Seems weeks

And for most
Beautiful
Rarest
of seconds

The noise
Stopped

Letting go

Leaves turn
From emerald shades
Fade to orange
Shaded to brown

Slowly dying
Yet still
Desperately
Holding on

Sheer will
To cling
Onto something

When the branch
Is shaking
Trying to release

Eager for new days
Soon waking

Yet that leave
Quaking
At the possibility
It's no longer needed

Feeds its fear
To let go
Be free
Of old tree
And grow anew

Love and Cheese – Shannon McEwen

Nomad

Just a small space
Of time
To reflect

To connect
With this woman
Here inside

Has she lost
Her place?

Will she finally
Open her heart
And confide?

Remove the shroud
Breathe in then out

I sit here
And wonder
If she'll ever be
What they see

Silly ways to try to love myself

The sun is peaking through
And I'm so in love with you
You've been with me

Right from the very start
You've got gumption
You've got heart

Sometimes you laugh
Like nothin's wrong
Sometimes you crumble
And just fall apart

Your pretty green eyes
Shinin' out amongst
Speckles of freckles

The sun is peaking through
And I'm so in love with you
You've been with me

Right from the very start
You've got gumption
You've got heart

Echoes of giggles
Promises of those
Happy little sighs

And hot tears that crawl
From days gone by
And I ain't gonna lie

She's scares me a bit
That little girl inside
Who's happy just because

Love and Cheese – Shannon McEwen

Maybe I'm most afraid
It'll never be as it was
Before she growed up

I suspect it's not that
But what I'd really be
If I just let go

The sun is peaking through
And I'm so in love with you
You've been with me

Right from the very start
You've got gumption
You've got heart

Being me

I wanna
Kick my legs
Push away
Close my eyes
And fly

I wanna
Giggle and grin
Remember
The simple joy
Once within

I wanna
Throw open
My arms
Without care
Of harm

I wanna
Just be me
Kicking
And free
In this swing

Love and Cheese – Shannon McEwen

Do I know you?

I know just a little
And everything
But mostly absolutely
Nothing at all
I know before you
Walked
You must have crawled
I know your smile
Sparkles
So very bright
And you probably
Sometimes feel sadness
In the aether of night
I know you stand out
And speak your mind
I get a great feeling
You're truly kind
I don't know
Where you're going
Or where you've been
I am uncertain
About all the things
You've seen
But I know
Somewhere in-between
Your smile
And incredible eyes
Lies a soul
With a whole lot
Goin' on

Renewals

Just after rain
Breathing in
Feels like rebirth

Free of smog
This brains fog
And politics and pain

Water slowly
Slowly
Drips
Rips through silence

Where for briefest
Of moments
The world seems
Sane

And I refrain
From constant train
Of thoughts

Savour this moment
For nothing but
Its unique existence

Despite
Deep resistance
Of all lain before

Outsourcing

May the sun
Kiss every inch
Of parched skin

Fill you
With only
Beautiful warmth
So deep within

And may
My love reach you
Somewhere
Inside that depth

So I may stop
Feeling
So very bereft

But even if
My brightness
Falls short

May you
Be filled with
Lightness
Of whichever love
You can

Finding her way

With every rapid beat
Of her very striking heart
Where old wood meets
One then two moving feet

Where she hears her soul
Seeks to find her whole
Somewhere on this trail
Between the shades of green

Where everything beautiful
Can so clearly be seen
Between where she began
And where it all ends

Her inner strength lends
A hand when she feels weak
And she can finally speak
Truth without pretend

Love and Cheese – Shannon McEwen

Sunday sunshine

I'm just a girl
On a Sunday
Morning train
Humming lyrics
To every
Happy refrain
Not even trying
To contain
This sparkle
In these green eyes
Breathing in deep
Then letting out
These happy sighs
The sun in my face
For the moment
Simply basking in
Quieted "why's"
Of life's hellos
Or goodbyes
Nor do I wonder
If it's at all wise
To sit and grin
As the miles
Fly by
Or that my
Smile is so wide
With no chagrin
I'm gonna just
Let it all in

Ashes

She rises
Despite relentless pain
Stretches, arches
Stands inside flames
Falters
Yet remains
Reborn

Love and Cheese – Shannon McEwen

Hold my own

I'd like to believe
I'm thoughtful
And Mostly kind

I've been told
Now and then
I've a beautiful mind

Out here in the cold
When I feel
Five years old

In the dark
Without a hand
To hold

I realize I must
Hold my own
Be my trust

While I whisper
Through soul
Blood and bone

I AM worthy
I am not alone
In my imperfectly
Beautiful mind

Empath

I want to wrap you
In my warm embrace
Wipe the tears
From your face

Stay until
You're a little
Less alone

Be your armour
When this world
Takes your best

And your reminder
Despite the pain
You're loved

Love and Cheese – Shannon McEwen

Be the love

Deep Inside this
Ever talking head
Inner voices murmur

A momentary pause
To decipher what was said
To discover the cause
Was me after all

Who cares if you're not ten feet tall
It harshly scolded
Be the love
You already know you are

If you can truly see
Before those voices
Gently folded
To silence once again

With the demons slain
Making it oddly plain
That to be the love

It's just as simple as
Releasing what the reaper sewed
And finally letting go

The beauty in snow

Cold snowdrops fall
Land with a soft plop
On the very top
Of red knitted head

Before tumbling
Fumbling
Mumbling
Before the landing
On upturned nose
In prayers pose

As beautiful flakes
Stake a claim
Reabsorbs
Into parched flesh

Cleanly mesh
Spirit with mind
A reminder where life
Is surely kind

With no need to rewind
But simply breathe
Leave the pain behind

Shapes in the clouds

From the ashes
Into a summer
Sunset

Disguised
As cloud
A Phoenix rises
Stretches
And circles

Leaving trails
Down warm cheeks
From the utter
Beauty
Of it all

Shades of foxes

Sultry eyes
Lined with black
Stare back
At me
From the
Skulk
Seductive
Deductive
Reduce me to tears
As they discover
All my fears
Here
In the henhouse
Where I laid
My eggs
And I paid
All of my dues
In hues of reds
And sad shades
Of blues
As I stand strong
Against
The tides
And the full moons
And whisper
To the monsters
In the dark
Please don't
Come back soon

Reflections of me

I looked in the mirror
Saw the delicate lines
Around my tired eyes
Built slowly over time

Then accompanied sighs
At the pockets of fat
And then tears
I silently, steadily cried

Until I looked closer
At the bags I saw there
Made that way
By all the care
I placed on my loves
And diligence of work
With the inner strength
That I stubbornly dare

I could see the smile
On my child's face
Where I could trace
Every deed I've done

And every extra mile
Until I came undone
And the bags grew
And before I knew

If I stood here now
In front of this glass
And saw only bad
Instead of class
And wouldn't it
Be so terribly sad
If I couldn't see truth
In my still vibrant youth?

The fight

My legs tremble
Hands shake
As I take
Another step

You'd think
It was a big
Decision

A milestone
Finally
Proudly
Conquered

Not the shaking
Of an everyday
Fight

To get out
Of bed

New ages

Like Humpty Dumpty
I tumbled
Fumbled
Finally fell

All the kings
Horses
And all of his men
Tried to piece me
Back together again

So the doc
Sewed me back
Together
With candy cane
Stitches
And the best wishes

And now
Here I am
I'm born Again
Like a renaissance
Woman

Curves
And curiosity
And love
In all the right places

Reflections of me

In the darkness
And the echo
Of children's laughter

Floating peacefully
On the surface
Of the lake

I sit
And quietly ponder
All I am
All I was
All I'll be

Despite the fact
That I cannot see

I'll have faith
In this
And in me

Love and Cheese – Shannon McEwen

Talkback

You, my darling girl
Are exquisitely flawed
In your imperfections
Your reflection
Not at all what you think

There are those
Who took your choice
And there are those
Who helped you find
Your beautiful voice

So my darling love
Let's rise above
This hatred of self
Because you
Are no longer the victim

But the warrior
Naked in vulnerability
Yet still so strong
Don't let this place
Get you down

You've not been wrong
Stand up and fight
With that killer smile
And sparkling eyes
Ignore the darkness

Turn those incredible sighs
From pain to pleasure
I'll even hold you
While you cry

Baring souls

Naked
I stand before
You

Arms open
Tears
Tumbling down

Knowing
What I am
Is imperfection

Desperately hoping
In the end
It'll be enough

Yet so scared
That despite
My immense love
It won't be

Love and Cheese – Shannon McEwen

Me

Because I see
Freedom
In this smile

All the while
Tired to marrow
Of bones

Hold me up
Crowded rooms
Yet oddly alone

Knowing I'd do
Anything despite
Miles to go

I am

Daydreamer
Deep emotion
Feeler

Wheeler and dealer
Of wisdom
And truth

Sharp tongue
Peeler
Of layers
Upon layers
Of lies that
Destroy youth

Unrepentant
Stealer
Of little moments
And big love

Unfortunate
Concealer
Of previous wrong
Ego and pride
Attempt to hide

With tough skin
Of pain within
And the softer side
That bares
My soul wide

Self-love manifesto

Love
No reservations
Required

Peaceful rest
When every part
Is soul tired

Perseverance
When darkness
Shades my heart

Courage
Until sanity
Is the last one
Standing

Freedom
To be inexplicably
Just me

Faith
To kill the pain
To be human
Instead of wraith
Once again

You are enough

It isn't profound
doesn't require
Eloquent monologue
Or constant praise

It isn't just a phase
Or clever phrase

But just
three little words
Whispered
Just so softly

Into the aether
Towards mine
Own reflection

Until self imposed
Infliction
Ceases to exist

And she's able
To resist
All other words

From the voices
In all directions
Inside one mind

Love and Cheese – Shannon McEwen

Who am I?

A woman stares through the reflection
Connects with my own eyes
Questions brimming like teardrops
Pools of green mixed with tiny brown flecks
Her dark hair frames her face
Attempts to hide her flaws
Her mouth parts
Words form, linger then stall
I find myself stepping back
Pausing
And looking with intent
At this woman standing before me
From head to toe
I peruse
Ponder
Wonder
And smile as I realize
I like this woman
With her wild hair and odd eyes
The freckles
Crooked smile
And way she looks back
Without pause, daring me to be

Part III: New Love

That elevator falling, spinning in circles until you fall down. thrill ride of new love feeling. There isn't anything like it.

A good feeling

An
Odd bliss
Bated breath
Lightness of heart
Incredible rush of adrenaline
Lips turn up with a simple thought of you
Sweet dreams linger
Souls entwined
In life's
Love

After the rain

Sweet moisture spills
A kamikaze plunge
From open skies
Before it lands
Then stills

Whispers wistful
Goodbyes
To the thrills
Settles in to nourish

Simple bud
Unaccomplished
Beauty in innocence
Hope in new blood
And honour
In old ties

But most of all
The love
That seeps in
Creeps along
Every silky petal

To begin
A new race
In a quiet space
To reveal life

Love and Cheese – Shannon McEwen

Afternoon walks

Sun shines off water
Creates a kind of light
Shimmers so brightly

In my tired soul
When you lift lips
To smile at me

Piece by piece
By ragged piece
Remakes me whole

Kisses my thirsty skin
Causes shivers
So deep within

And the darkness
That took its toll
Shrivels just a bit

Alive again

What is this pitter
              patter of my heart?
The skip and dance
          and slow entrance
Music playing
  In an occupied mind

Every nerve stretches
            blinks and wakes
Cold veins defrost
   Blood races to find
The reasons
     Behind the sudden smile

What is this feeling
          that grips me?
The urge
    To find out every detail
A mind that wanders
                Plays and imagines

Every cell tickles
              Throbs,
                    tingles
Cold flesh melts
When eyes connect

Electricity
          Brings me
Alive once again

Love and Cheese – Shannon McEwen

Eye contact

She spies him
A second before he does
Takes time to trace his face
Love every inch with her eyes

Angular jaw line
Five o'clock shadow
A slight bend along the ride
In an otherwise perfect profile

Without warning he turns
A gaze returned
Deep shades of blue
A jaunty sparkle
Lips turn upward with ease
She feels a pump
       Pump
        Pumping

As the blood in her veins revs up
    Takes off
     Traces
      Races
Breakneck speeds
Spreads liquid warmth
Into every pore

Before - whoosh!
She exhales slowly
Inhales
Sweet air
Yet she remains breathless
Spirits rise
    Up
     Up
Bubble to the surface
Escape

In this moment
She is alive.

Always Saturday

Monday came and before I knew
Tuesday had whittled away
Wednesday flew
Thursday sped
Friday disappeared
Saturday fled
Until I saw you
I remain hopeful
Sunday will not come
With proof
Of too good to be true

Be mine

Fingers linked
In firm connection
Sweet confection
Of loving lips

Hip to hip
From inner depth
Entwined souls

Tingle down
From brain
To breast

Through blood
And bone
To tips of toes

Nourishes me
Until I'm whole
So blissfully full
Feeds all I need

Beautiful souls

Where the rays
Meet the waves

Create a thing
Of beauty

I'm reminded
Of where your soul
Meets mine

And I know
It's just as divine

Here I sigh
Wipe profound tears
From these eyes

Because beauty
Of the image
Before me
And within me

Quantum entanglement

Somehow you
Got tangled
So deeply
Inside of me

Until impossible
To separate
The very particles
Of root from tree

Infinitesimal
Bits of debris
From my soul
To the parts that
make you whole

Left to see
This beautiful
Quantum
entanglement

Between the lines

I'm here baby
Thinkin' of you
Loving
Outta the blue

Memories
Of kisses
And wistful wishes
With passion too

Freedom sought
Between
The mundane
And utterly insane

Where you and me
Only see
The space between
Our hearts
And these eyes

Measured by
Satiated cries
And the happiest
Of sighs

In a place
Where this love
Just cannot
Die

Bubble baths and beautiful thoughts

After chaos
Blessed darkness
Except a flicker of wick
And the faint scent of cranberry

I close my tired eyes
Let Warm water
Ever so slowly
caress
Away the tension

Until nothing remains of the day
But the beautiful thought

Of you.

Call me a hypocrite but a happy one

I protest
The meaning
Industry creates
For profit
Of love

Until I open the card
Skip the strategically
Typed hype
See
Your words

Printed in blue ink
"My love, my passion, my conviction, I love you"

And I melt
Like butter
and let the shortbread
Go straight to my thighs

Industry be damned
because I believe

How many more sleeps?

Sitting here watching day
Fade to night
A tree all decorated
With festive light

Laughter
And excitement
surround
From the days activity

You far away
And me here
So I close my eyes
Wipe the water
That leaks with these sighs

And I picture the quiet scene
Sugar cookies and tea
And you
And me

Not unlike that night
Not so long ago
Where we sat and spoke
And my heart awoke
Some way through

The conversations, laughter
And crumbs
And sips of tea
Of you and me

Camping in the rain

Let's just lay
Listen to raindrops
Plop
  Plop
    Plop

Onto the fabric
Of our little tent
Stay right here

Until we're spent
Cuddle me near
Devoid of fear

Just sweet nothing
But you and me
Nestled so snugly

In this cocoon
Warm and dry
Except in all
The right places

Candlelight

The flame licks
As it flicks its light
Makes a shadow
Into the darkest night

Stretches, fills and warms
A cold soul
As slowly ivory wax drips
Grips
   slips
Creates a romantic illusion
Shines a soft haze
In an oasis of dreams
Sweet scent heats
Releases its power

Surrounds, teases, feeds
Senses with desire
Seeds of sorrow
Wither as soft light embraces

A time of no tomorrow
A moment borrowed
No regrets
  No angry faces
Just a lovely glow
Melts a tired heart
From ragged binds
Rewinds chaos
  Erases pain
and encases

A silent soul
  Stolen moment to console
A second in the whole
    For candlelit reflection

Music to my ears

There's music in my ears
And I'm swaying
With the movement
Of the morning train
Thinking about my baby
And my smile just keeps
Getting wider and wider
And I must confide
This feeling inside
Just keeps getting
brighter and brighter
Thinking about my baby
And my smile just keeps
Getting wider and wider
The crowds are pushing in
But I don't care
I'm singing along
To the song in my heart
Grinning like a fool
A bright light
In the dull greyness
Of morning commute
There's no disputes
Thinking about my baby
And my smile just keeps
Getting wider and wider

Lip balm not required

His smile
Cracks the facade
Of the mask I once wore
Clean air rushes through beloved
Lips touch

Sipping tea under a tin roof

Fat raindrops fall
Tumble down
Plink,
  plink
   plink
Musically
onto tin roof

Before it slips
Slowly down
Drips
to the ground
Soaks into earth

Like your eyes
Into my soul
Look down
Into me

So thirsty
In this storm
We've created

Recharging the batteries

I can't get through
And I panic
Because I can't see
Your beautiful face
Hear your beautiful voice
Connect
With your soul
So I can plug in
To once again
Feel whole
Across the lines
Where we collide
Until the physical
Can once again unite
Excite the senses
Touch of fingertips
Lip to Lip
Sip - Of your love
Not just whispers
Across cables
Able to keep
This ache at bay
Persuade this heart
That all's well
While half is missing
And pulled apart
A reminder
It's truly an art
This juggling of logic
And emotion
And what draws us
So close together
Isn't always obvious
When we can't
Touch it – See it – Feel it
Except in our hearts

Cycling my thoughts to you

On this very non-descript dull day
Way beyond my physical touch

Much of "you" clings to most of me
Seeing you in my every other thought
Ought to make you smile in your dreams

Seems like I'm just a little addicted
Fed a constant diet of your beautiful light
Right in the midst of constant chaos

Lost between where I am and you sleep
Keeping my body in constant need
Leading my mind back to you

Beautiful souls

The words drip
So beautifully
from the tip of your pen

Reverberate from lungs
Dance off tongue
Before sung from lips

With soft vulnerability
Yet quiet strength
About wonders
Dark corners
Strife

A good mans choices
And the small insights of life
Strung together

By melodies
Lyrics
And emotions
And infinitesimal bits
Of your soul

Woven throughout
Bound together
To trick this listener
Into feeling whole

Letters

Words etched
Into the parchment

straight
from your heart
to mine

soaked
in sincerity

Salted drops
drip
down cheeks

from the utter beauty
of the message

Wraps around me
like a warm
hug

Dandelion wishes

Lips purse, air rushes
Gently then quickly
Passionately brushes

With life's sweet touch
Tickles every fibre
Until it becomes too much

White cotton wishes
From the centre explode
Lightens the load

In a solitary heart
Where sunshine kisses
Every single inch

And a beautiful song
From a hopeful soul
Know these wishes
Can't go wrong

Days of worship

Schools of fishes
Swim in patterns
Between fingers
Dipping into current

And reams
Of wistful wishes
Slip off my tongue
To Softly linger

Like traces
Of little kisses
Placed upon
Sun warmed skin

Evoking elation
Somewhere
So deep within
Somehow akin

A willing sacrifice
To Brigid
And inspiration
Of long lost
Worship of a
Goddess

Dreaming of you

Snuggled into covers
sighing as cool air
From the fan

Brushes ever
So Softly across
Exposed face

Almost like the brush
Of hand
Traced across skin,

Until every tiny hair
Stands to attention
And dances

Fantastical worlds

Sweetest dreams
Of kisses
And wishes
That all come true

Of cotton candy clouds
And only skies
Of the brightest blue

Where somewhere
In the distance
Is me
And you

Smiles so wide
It's so impossible
To hide

And we can confide
In the suns truth
Wise in all life's ties

Minds full of youth
Warriors
And goddesses
Reside

And love
Pure love
Cannot lie

First glances

Lungs expand
Draw in first taste
Of new days' air

Clouds sprinkle
Distant horizon
Yet cannot cover

The sneak peek
Of pigment
that dances

Merrily prances
Across the sky
And through
My thirsty heart

Daybreak filled
With such
Splendid possibility

Flyin' away

Let's fly away baby
To a faraway place
We can live on love
In a magical space

Where warmth
Closes miles
Breaks out smiles
On my baby's
Beautiful face

Let's fly away baby
To a faraway place
And leave it all be
With nothin'
To carry except
You and me

Then we'll see
Bluest skies
Mingled with
My happy sighs

We'll get it right
On the first try
Let's fly away baby
To a faraway place

Good night moon

Much needed hush
Dim shadows loom
After a day filled rush

His voice fills the room
Washes away the gloom
As I lay and listen

Every nerve comes to call
More pieces of me fall
This love in my ear

Wipes away these fears
Makes me feel at least
Ten glorious feet tall

Hand in hand

Take my hand
And we'll fly to the moon
You'll dance with the fork
And I'll dance with the spoon

We'll listen to the man
Softly, softly croon
Whispering lyrics
Slightly out of tune

Take my hand
And we'll fly to the moon
I'll kiss you silly and
We'll lovingly cocoon

And we won't be back
Anytime soon
We'll just sit and ponder
Until the hour of noon

Take my hand
And we'll fly to the moon
Let our hearts be immune
To uncertainties typhoon

Take my hand
So we can fly away
Until the month of May
It'll be grand

In a psychedelic cartoon
We'll so happily stay
And for once the love
Will have the last say
So take my hand
And we'll fly to the moon

Love and Cheese – Shannon McEwen

Hidden beaches

Lush green trees
Open succulent arms
Reveal what our love sees
In this surreal beauty

Our own little oasis
Where our smiling faces
Can press together
In breathtaking embrace

Where sand stretches
From lavish treeline
To where water laps
And the sun fetches

Every vibrant beam
Sensually stretches
Make green eyes gleam
Love from you to me

I love you

I know they say
The words
Are nothing
But words

I've been told
Show
Not tell

But I can't seem
To stop
The words

From bouncing
Across my tongue
Before they
Slide along my enamel

And slip
From chapped lips

Love and Cheese – Shannon McEwen

Finding faith from a distance

Always Wednesday
Stuck in a loop
Emotions droop
I press the button
Make the call
But nothing happens
It all falls
Into the abyss
Of the black hole
Wifi darkness
Starkness
Where somewhere
Between here
And there
We've been
Disconnected
So we must reach
Out of ourselves
Off of these shelves
And think beyond
Logic and emotion
To faith
Teach our souls
To trust in each other
And in what we already know
If we still our minds
And slow our hearts
Come somewhat apart
To come together again
So we can find
Love is surely bright
Right here within
Beneath the chaos
Self created
If we simply lift it
To the light

In his eyes

In his eyes I see
Such beautiful images
Of who I want to be

Without nagging qualm
Just me as I wholly am
His faith a soothing balm

In his eyes I am
So much more than I know
Where beauty is me

I have no further to go
The courage to grow
And I can take it slow

In his eyes I shine
Far brighter than I do
Where life is mine

Where I dance in time
And sing in line
Despite reality's climb

In his eyes I am love
I see, I am, I shine
All because he's mine

Love and Cheese – Shannon McEwen

Impromptu meditations

Floating along
So gently
With the waves

Made from speedboats
And children
Jumping into the cove

As my hand dips
Into cool water
To glide just beneath
The surface

Sun glints
Off the silver
Of the Claddagh
On my finger

And in this
Beautiful moment
I think of you

In your smile

Inside your smile
And in your eyes
I could go for miles

Before I nestled in
To stay a while
Listen to nothing
But your happy sighs

Taste of your lips
Mingled so nicely
With satiated cries

Bask in the light
From your soul
To my old heart
So incredibly bright

Despite the scars
Miraculously mends
To make me whole

Love and Cheese – Shannon McEwen

Smiles to you

A twitch
At the right
Corner of my mouth

Where you like
To take the very tip
Of your finger

And coax my smile
When I don't
Feel like it

Except this time
Just the thought
Of you
Does the trick

Just a smile

With absolutely nothing
But your brilliant smile
A tiny tingle starts
At the end of my little toe

Grows as it travels
Unravels
Slowly then swiftly
Up a thigh, hip, my lips

To breast where underneath
The beat, beat, beating
At the centre of my being
Does a happy little flip

Languages of love

Bodies press
Desperately wrestle
Pressure builds

Patience redress
Until I confess
That I need help

And it pains
To truly admit
But hope remains

Rescue comes
kindness reigns
With redemption

A white knight
In a blue taxi
And all is right

Let's monkey around

Let's monkey around
Drown out the sound
Except the giggles
And the wiggles
And the glee

As we bounce
        Trounce
           Flounce
Across the world
Then back again
Swing from tree
          To tree
      To swinging tree

Let's not think
Just be
You
And me

Throwing kisses
And crazy, whirlwind
Kamikaze wishes
Without fear
I'll hold you near

So let's monkey around
And around
And around
Let the fun abound
Let's get lost
And not be found

Love of art

Words appear
Here on this page
In concert
With every stroke

Of your
Brightly hued brush
Lushly spread
Bristles rush

Across canvass
Before inevitably
Your art
Covers the whole
Of my heart

Love rains on me

Fat drops rapidly fall
Early morning showers
Through open windows

I comfortably lay
Snuggled in your arms
Sheltered from harm

Where every time I wake
Your face so close to mine
Our hearts beat in time

To the raindrops that fall
Where I give you my all
And you look into my eyes

Smile at my sighs
And call me on all my lies
To love me just because

Love and Cheese – Shannon McEwen

Lovers stroll

Setting sun, we walk
While comfortably talk
Like we're beautifully
And so fully in tune

Between fading light
And the rising moon
Such incredible sight
Your hand in mine

As day turns to night
And it's your love
Warms me bright
Your sweet soul

That holds me tight
Makes me whole
As we go in shadow
On a lover's stroll

Making love to the music

Such delight
Washes over me
Stirs every cell
Feels every note
Of what's being played

My emotions
Laid bare
Happiness displayed
In a world where
I've naught a care
Instead of usual
Buyer beware

And the sun peaks
Seeks the warmth
Of my skin
Somewhere within
So deep it hides

Until the music
Soulfully listens
Until my heart
Softly confides

Mastery

Eloquent mastery
Entwined in souls
Made whole
Simply by being

By seeing
Infinite emotions
Wrapped in logic
Cause commotion

Beautiful chaos
Where once empty
Fill with devotion
To new religion

Lessen indecision
Blows kisses
Once scattered
Sudden precision

Explosive fission
Lives entangled
Brilliant epiphany
Knowing I mattered

Messages

Just words on a page
Keyed lovingly
From you to me

Swoop in
Cradle my heart
Illuminate my soul

Imagery meant to
Make me whole
Help me see

The light
From your eyes
To mine

Midday dreams

Inside this face
Every single
Thinking space
Is filled to capacity
with thoughts
Of you

All the kisses
And near misses
Adventure driven
Wistful wishing
We do

Where we smile
And dream
Of reams
And reams
And reams

That life will
Be better
Than this moment
Seems

And these miles
That separate
It all
Will slowly
Slowly
Fall away

More than that

I love you
In the morning
Through afternoon
I love you
Even more
Than the man
In the moon

I love you better
Than the cow
The fork
Dish and spoon
Here and now
I softly croon

This love I have
Isn't leaving
Anytime soon
So let's dance
To a much
Happier tune

I love you
From the morning
And every
Single hour
Of every night
Until I blink
And see light

Do you love me
As much as that?

Love and Cheese – Shannon McEwen

Doubt dissolves

Candlelight reflects in your eyes
Gives me a perfect view
Of your soul
And my doubt dissolves
In your gaze
In your arms
In your heart

In your love
I realize the folly of my doubt
You did not break my heart
Or my trust

Instead
You wash away the pain
The fear
And fill me with such unbelievable love
When you look into my eyes

Next kiss

Three hundred and sixty-five days

Eight thousand seven hundred
Sixty-three and one quarter hours

Five hundred twenty-five thousand
Six hundred and nine seconds

A recount of the time
From our first kiss

And only three hours
Fourteen minutes
Two and one third seconds
Since I kissed you
Came to work
And began counting down

Love and Cheese – Shannon McEwen

None

Hushed warm embrace of flickering light
Where every burden is left at the door
Met with naught but this exquisite sight

Where every soft touch feels just right
Without a plan and nobody keeps score
Hushed warm embrace of flickering light

Briefly chases away darkness of night
Tensions slowly scattered on the floor
Met with naught but this lovely sight

I let it all go and simply hold on tight
Glad being with you is never a chore
Hushed warm embrace of flickering light

The look in your eyes makes things bright
Washes away deep fear in my very core
Met with naught but this exquisite sight

Taking this moment not feeling contrite
Wishing time would give just a little more
Hushed warm embrace of flickering light
Met with naught but this exquisite sight

Play with me

Let's stay in bed
Waste the day
Eat with our fingers
In between play

Let feathers fly
As we nap away
The hours
Slowly ticking by

With little kisses
And no need
For penny wishes
That already
Came true

Blue skies
And candy clouds
Can't shroud
This playful day
Where we laugh

Then come undone
Cut
Worries by half
Mingled with
Whispered stories
And nothing
But fun

Love and Cheese – Shannon McEwen

Pondering you

Sitting in the dark
With only my contemplations
To spark

This unhurried thought
Where there is me
Mixed with you

Nothing left to ponder
For this moment
Except to simply be

Me
Mixed with you
Here in my head

Respite

Darkness blankets us
The moon, a tiny night light
In a backdrop of stars

That lend to the melody
Of you
And me

Mingled Limbs
And tangled hearts
Take brief respite

Wait for sunlight to soak
Through shaded panes
Into the flesh of our love

Love and Cheese – Shannon McEwen

Reminders of you

I hear our song
Instantly
My lips lift
And stretch wide

There isn't any way
I can hide
This sparkle
In my eyes

Or the love
That rushes
Through veins
To my heart
My brain

To where my soul
Is fully entangled
With yours

Sitting here amidst the calm

Sitting here amidst the calm
Softly tracing upon my palm

Knowledge in the bigger scheme
Problems smaller than they seem

Thinking thoughts of random fields
As layers of truth get revealed

To tell me what it truly means
Beyond these daily silly scenes

That life means more than what I see
Quite simply you may be the key

Snotty love

I cried tears onto the grey of your shirt
Big, fat, salty drops
Mingled with snot
Smudges of black mascara
And the gunk from the corner
Of red swollen eyes

A sniffle
A sigh
A deep breath

Until your scent seeped
Past the snot
Into my consciousness
And the tears, the snot and the lies
Washed away
left with only you

Soothe Sayers

Cool fingertips
Softly slip
Across soft skin
That encases
Aching pain within

Faces pressed
Close together
Barest brush
Of softest lips

Heartbeat flips
Kamikaze flops
Threatens again
To finally stop
As distance reigns

Blown kisses
Followed closely
By ragged wishes
Of warm hands
That take hold
Of stories told

Summer winds

I will always
Always
Always
Think of you

Your whispered
Love
Drift gently
Across my soul

Your words
Your sweet
Sweet
Words

Once thought
To be wind
Curl around me
To make me whole

Stay with me
Ensconced
From the dark

Let your thoughts
And kisses
And words
Find their mark

Sunsets and moments

Skies turn from bright blue
Fade to a softer hue
Before shades of pink
In the blink

Of these tired eyes
And my peaceful sighs
As I lie
Here wrapped in you

Breathe in the air
See every shade of green
In the blades of grass
Where we lay

And nothing to say
Without doubt
It's going to be okay
As our hearts beat

Defeat the fear
One moment at a time
Sublime
From loving you

Smiling on the Train

Black outside the glass
As if teardrops
Fall down
Down
Down
The cold panes

In wild fall refrains
As I sit here
On the train
But instead of sadness
Where I'd usually descend
I find myself
Smiling at my own
Reflection

Because this smile
Brings me the miles
Back to you

And the warmth
Of your eyes
Where your own smile
Creeps
From edges of lips

Before it slips
Across cheeks
Into the beautiful seas
Of your eyes

And sparkles there
Before it shoots
Back at me
Until I can't
Possible help
But smile back

Sushi

At the table with two broken chairs
Salmon maki and California roll
And the miso soup that spills
Out of the white Styrofoam bowl
Onto the green cotton fabric of my tee shirt
Followed by the laughter
And the smiles
Along with the love
I see in your eyes
At my finest moments

Love and Cheese – Shannon McEwen

The flow of us

The beauty in movement
Between yours and mine
So incredibly sublime

The touch, the kiss
The lingering look
Loves ever tender hook

Pulls every nerve within
From tip of baby toe
To the depths of my soul

Where I find you and me
Wrapped in life's pleasure
And where I can truly be

The pitter-patter of you

The soft plunking of rain
Against windshield
Reminds me strikingly

The rapid pitter-patter
Of my heart
When you're near

Where fear has no space
In this beautiful place
Only vibrant life

Rife
With delight
In every fibre of being

Even in the absolute
Absence
Of light

The room seduced by shadows

Shadows of us
Move across the room
Made large by a small flame
That bends and sparkles
In an otherwise dark room

Dances to the music
That croons
From the twin speakers

Sober Sentinels
Pretend indifference to the ballad
That course
Through their innards

On the nondescript beige wall
Two gigantic shadow figures
Become one

Even the sentinels
can't hide their smiles

and my heart
beats,
thump,
   thump,
      thump
faster than then ballad.

The sunshine of you

To see that stunning smile
Lift your cheeks
Spread across your face
And onto mine

Just because you're near
Washes away the fear
With the laughter
Sparkling like diamonds

Between the spaces
And the many faces
The glow that seeps inside
From darkness light replaces

All because of you
And the happiness
You so gloriously
Completely, Exemplify

Love and Cheese – Shannon McEwen

There you are

It isn't gratitude
Or pretty
Platitudes

It isn't kisses
And whispered
Bedtime wishes

It isn't touch
Or taste
Nor melodic sound
Outta the blue

Where I've found
My ground
In this love for you

But the look
From your eyes
To mine
That speaks
In perfect time

Thoughts of you

In the eerie light
Of the crescent moon
I look up
See its ethereal beauty
And think
Of you.

Love and Cheese – Shannon McEwen

Waiting for redemption

Every moment
Spent with phone
Clutched in hand

Waiting
Wanting
Begging it to beep

To send me
Infinitesimal pieces
Of you

To fill these cracks
Here in my soul

Where what seems
Like an eternity ago
You made me feel whole

Who cares about clichés

We can write of flowers
Of buds, of petals, princesses
Locked in their shaded bowers

The vivid image of life's woes
Tears, fears, anger and pain
Accepted words of modern prose

Just when did it become taboo?
To write three simple words
"I love you"

How exactly should one convey
And when did love
Become a jaded cliché?

Love and Cheese – Shannon McEwen

Wistful wishes

Let's throw up arms
Faces pressed
To glorious sun

Spin in circles
Until we're undone
Release this fear

Turn our ears
To the sounds
Of our pleasure

Take no measure
Of outside pain
Feel free again

Only this love
To guide us
Safely home

With you

It's not a matter
Of sorting through
Old memories
Rather the anticipation
Of making fresh ones

It's never
What you can do
For me
But how well we do things
Together

There is nothing to be said
That could even begin
An accurate description
Of how full my heart feels
With you

Love and Cheese – Shannon McEwen

Blanket forts and rainy days

Let's build a fort
Out of blankets
Make a sport
Out of cuddles
Soaked in puddles
And puddles
Of tears
That drip down our faces
Made only of laughter
Or the miles
Upon miles
Of smiles
That fill all of the spaces
Like sunshine
In this otherwise rainy day
Where happiness
Made with love
Keeps any sad thoughts
Firmly at bay
A remedy
Full of giggles
And wiggling limbs
Where we can't tell
Whose feet are whose
And where either
Of us ends or begins
From this pile
Here in our blanket fort
A panda standing guard
At the door
Of our secret hideaway
And where this place
Is filled with so
Much love
Here today

You

In this shaded mind
I like to press rewind
And replay
Again and again
And yet again
Every moment
With you

Love and Cheese – Shannon McEwen

Your arms

In your arms I find myself in love
Incredible emotion fills my heart
A faint cry of angels high above
In your arms I find myself in love
Minds entwined like hand in glove
Gazes locked I feel the fear depart
In your arms I find myself in love
Incredible emotion fills my heart

You're like the sun

The moment
Light filters through
Dust particles

Gold rays
Stretch and flick
Across cool cheek

And I longingly lift
My face another inch
To feel the warmth

And the worship
Of something
So beautifully bright

Cravings

Since the moment
Your eyes
Kissed mine

The very texture
Of the air
Between us changed

And I knew
Life would never
Be the same
Without you

So my heart
Reached quickly
Out to entwine

Pulled you in
And it felt
So incredibly divine

And continues
To hungrily crave
Every single
Moment with you

Enchantment

Eyes sparkle
And dance like
Enchanted lights

Snow lit mazes
Whispered wishes
Fevered kisses
Taste of mulled wine

And trace of skin
Touches
so deep within

Like a celestial hand
Reaches
Through stardust

Brushes finger tips
Down his soul

And that rare
feeling
Of being whole

Part IV: Enduring Love

The difference between infatuation and love is that one is fleeting while the other persists though tested time and again. Somewhere between the messy and the mundane, real love endures.

After the fireworks but before the parade

Heated kisses and soul searing hugs
Zealous lust the years have tamed
Fireworks turn to less frequent tugs

Where the clock ticks and time shrugs
Looks to memories of lovers famed
Heated kisses and soul searing hugs

Stranded on faded heart shaped rugs
Feeling the momentum softly flamed
Fireworks turn to less frequent tugs

A hectic life where responsibility lugs
Love remains but so often unnamed
Heated kisses and soul searing hugs

Time steals moments like juvenile thugs
Still a heart remains so tightly claimed
Fireworks turn to less frequent tugs

A moment with you so fully drugs
And love is once again aptly renamed
Heated kisses and soul searing hugs
Fireworks turn to less frequent tugs

And still

Inside the space
Between
This beautiful
embrace

Where faces
Pressed together
And hearts beat
In unison

In the heat
Of time stood still
We take our fill

And still
Realize it could
Never be enough

Be your strength

Put your head on my shoulder
And let it all out
Put your hand in mine
No matter what it's about

I'll love you today
And I'll love you tomorrow
I'll love you until
All the earths blown away

Put your head on my shoulder
And let it all out
Put your hand in mine
No matter what it's about

I'll be your strength
When yours is all gone
I'll be your voice
Until the curtains are drawn

Put your head on my shoulder
And let it all out
Put your hand in mine
No matter what it's about

Place your faith in mine
When the hands of time
Make it hard to breathe
And life so hard to climb

Put your head on my shoulder
And let it all out
Put your hand in mine
No matter what it's about

Scream, vent or shout
Until your tears turn to a sigh
And your smile finally comes out

Put your head on my shoulder
And let it all out
Put your hand in mine
No matter what it's about

Love and Cheese – Shannon McEwen

Between Insanity and bliss

Money issues
Stacks upon stacks of Dirty Dishes
Daily hour-long commutes
Never ending custody dispute

Looks like rain
The world's gone insane
Out of milk
And short of time

Darkness comes
Nothing's ever done
Kids finally tucked in bed

On your lap
I rest my head
With a gentle hand
You fill the gap

Bright moments

Our song came on
In the middle
Of my day

And for a moment
It took me
So very far away

From the stress
And chaos
Fluorescent lights
And daily fray

Right into your arms
Head rested
On your shoulder
As we swayed

I closed my eyes
Held on tight
Before it ended
And then I sighed

But for that
Brief glimpse
Everything in my world
Was right

Broken Wings

And still
From the first flutter
Of eye lashes

Until closing
Tired green eyes
And every moment
In between

It's you
Always you

Even when
These angel wings
Clipped

Slipped from slumped
Shoulders
Too weak to bear

Inevitable discovery
Of imperfection
Fall to ashes

Calling me home

Home isn't
Wood or stone
Or things
And rings

Home is
Blood and bone
Where the love
Keeps you
From being alone

And forever
Sets the tone
Of not just
Where I rest my head

But where what's
Beneath breast
And beyond brain

Entwines
And combines
To create this feeling
Of utter peace

Love and Cheese – Shannon McEwen

Chapped lips

And in this moment
Peace washes
Over my scars

Where nothing
But this feeling
Matters

And this thought
Seemingly mundane
Of you

And simple life
Where we talk
And laugh
And live

Where nothing else
Seems to matter
But the smile

That spreads
All because of you

Cheesy Sentiments

Where once the light could not stroke
In the many shadows inside my heart
When life had played another cruel joke
The darkness you've since helped tear apart

Your quiet love shone right on through
Past the shards and between the tears
Changing old clichés to something new
Slowly erasing all my former fears

A kiss, a look, a smile, a laugh
Your solid strength around my soul
Simple words don't explain by half
How this could possibly make me whole

Close the curtains

Forget that in the daylight
Obligation claims us
Concern of the unknown
Clenches
Our hearts

Until breathing is painful
And the doubt
Seeps in

Let's close the curtains
And turn down the bed

Light a candle
Before you hold me tight

Kiss away
  The worry
Touch away
   The pain
Until there is nothing

But you
And I
In love.

Cuddle up to you

Sunshine peaks
Boldly sneaks
Through dusty panes
The ache slowly wanes

As I roll into you
And the shine
From your eyes
To mine
Wipes away the blue

Your fingers brush
Through my hair
Rush across skin
Shoot all worries
Into the air

Obliterated swiftly
By happy little sighs
Followed shortly
By even happier
Little cries

Love and Cheese – Shannon McEwen

Desktop photo

In the harsh light of
Fluorescent bulb

You stand and smile
From behind the glass

Resplendent
Not because of the tuxedo

But the smile
That begins at the very edge

Of your lips
And spreads upwards

Until it reaches your eyes
And emanates from every pore

And I'm blinded by
Your brilliance

And immersed
In you

Dreams spinning

In sweet repose, dreams we lay spinning
In the early light of a rainy August day
Cotton dreams of life's constant sinning
In sweet repose, dreams we lay spinning
Free of anger ready for a new beginning
The nightmares of old begin to fade away
In sweet repose, dreams we lay spinning
In the early light of a rainy August day

Eclipse

A shadow cast upon the moon
In silky satin shades of crimson
Translucent in its glory
Ethereal in its beauty
And in that moment
I thought of you
And realized the eclipse
Could not compare
To the brilliance of you

Eternal is

Eternal is the night, infernal is the fright
And the fleeing sense of right
As the dream turns cold
Filled with fleeting images
  Raw feelings
    Days of old
      Horrors told
As My fears rapidly unfold

Eternal is the day my soul entwined
Our love combined
  We began the journey
 Through the heart
    Embedded so deeply
   Our love may falter
But will never die
    Tears I cry, at times I sigh
But even with broken wings
  Hope will always fly

Eternal is a spirit that soars alone
  Roars through flesh and bone
Unique, beautiful, a love
      Vividly Alive
        Tenacious - survive
Unstoppable even in dire straits
  When darkness waits
Until fear abates

Love and Cheese – Shannon McEwen

Even if

Nothing else changed
But the passing of time
Nothing was created
No reasons or rhymes

Dreams evaporated
Into nothing but dust
Every goal became chain
That grew covered in rust

And life stayed the same
In exactly every way
I would be truly blessed
Each and every day

While its fun to imagine
And even better to dream
Even if none of it remained
You and I are a team

Dreams are dreams
That defines me too
But If I had to choose
I would always choose you

Expansions of the heart

Let's entwine hearts
Like these fingers
And be aware

To always take care
Of yesterday's lessons
Love and memories

To bring forward
To new love
Where we combine
Our lives
Respecting

Expecting
Reflecting the beauty
Of from where we came
Never the same

Family
Roots expanding
Flame
Never extinguished

Simply burning
Yearning
In the beautiful eyes
Of our children

Love and Cheese – Shannon McEwen

Everywhere I see is you

In the towel
I always place
Just for you

In the scent
Of the body butter
On my damp skin

In the colours
Reflecting
In this candlelight

And the memory
Of your arm
Pressed around
Me tight

From the song
Softly playing
On my phone

And how it makes
Me feel
Just a little less alone

Expressions

Despite every
Letter
Language
Or line

Number, Symbol
And sign
There just isn't
Enough
To explain

Just how much
You mean
To me

Gypsy Love

Green silk scarf
Against the shine
Of dark hair

Backdrop
For these green eyes
Sending love

From me to you
Through this
Sunshiny July air

As laughter swells
And dances
At the summer fair

And this love
This vibrant love
I can always see
In your face
There

Hanging on

I'll wipe your tears
In this beautiful place
Once called hell

I'll never tell
I'll just embrace
The very tips
Of your wary soul

And hang tight
Until
You feel whole

And truth be told
Here in the cold
I'll be the warmth
Until the sun
Takes hold

Love and Cheese – Shannon McEwen

How I know

It isn't the big events
Grand gestures
Declarations
Or public displays

But the way
You pull me close
Run your long fingers
Softly
Rhythmically
Along my scalp

Just because I like it

How to explain you

To the first opening of my eyes
Ever mingled with daily chaos
Down to the very last of my sighs

The solid sense of you beside
Betwixt every sun and moon
A place where I truly reside

The next breath that is held
Savoured and then released
As if somehow compelled

And no words to truly explain
From the start of time to forever
I would do it all with you again

Love and Cheese – Shannon McEwen

I think

I think I loved you yesterday
And then again today
And I will love you
All of tomorrow if I may

I think I saw your smile
In my deepest dream
Delectable like strawberries
With whitest, thickest cream

I think your charms
Have done me in for good
In your arms pleasure
Is most certainly understood

I think my heart is melting
In your steady gaze
A kaleidoscope
Of such wondrous haze

Please tell me
This is not just a silly phase

I think I'll keep you
Forever and one day
If I can hold on
Not ever let you go

But I will love you
Even if you slip
Slip away

Important snapshots of life

A simple,
Insignificant moment
An uneventful
Morning commute

Nothing but traffic
Morning sun peeking out
Between fluffy clouds
And sporadic yawning

Except the laughter
Then Silly utterings
And juvenile taunting
Over a wrong turn

Before the incredible grin
That warmly spread
From your lips, to your eyes
To my soul

Insomnia

Lights switch off
Brain turns on
Thoughts bombard
Peace is gone

Soothing swishing
Of the fan
Yet still I cannot
Find the shut off
My wired mind

Thoughts
And images
Old memories
To reluctantly find

Leaving nothing
Unturned
Too wholly true
To be really kind

Yet meander
To the bright, sunny
Spot I've got
So full of you

Just a glance

Despite any pain
We sometimes
Inflict

I wanna tell you
Regardless of any
Conflict

Every single time
I so much as glance
Into those
Endless eyes

All over again
To my surprise
I stumble
And fall

Back into you
And that soul soaked
Map
Our hearts drew

Just because

For no other
Ulterior motives
Apologies
Big events
Or reasons

Just a token
Love sent
From you
To me

Outta the blue
So I can see
I was thought of
Held above
The daily grind

Great expectations

In the unlikeliest moments
When least expected
The most incredible things
A life
Can bring

Darkened room
Where bitter gloom
Has washed all the air
From lungs
But the voice
On the other end
Of the line

Breathes
Life back into
Mine

In the unlikeliest moments
When least expected
The most incredible things
A life
Can bring

In the moment
Where the worlds
Stopped spinning
And nothing
Seems to be winning

Your hand
Slips into mine
And you softly whisper
It's going to be just fine

Love and Cheese – Shannon McEwen

In the unlikeliest moments
When least expected
The most incredible things
A life
Can bring

My heart beats
And yours responds
No matter the call

Whether I fly
Or you fall

The sun, the moon
The stars
The simple beauty
Of it all

In the unlikeliest moments
When least expected
The most incredible things
A life
Can bring

Knowledge transfer

In the darkness
And the light
You've been
My real-life hero
My love
My knight

Who despite
Your very own battles
Took up
My plight

When blind
With fear
Give me sight

And always
Never fail
Work to make
It right.

A lesson
That love
Isn't the shiny things
Or always bright

But the simple act
Of wiping my tears
In the horrors
Of night

Holding my hand
When nobody would

Love and Cheese – Shannon McEwen

Taking my pain in
Again
And again
And again

Never letting
Me accept
Really old shame

Seeing me beautiful
At my very worst
And knowing
Without any words
To hold me first

That, my soulmate
Is what love is
Which of course
You already knew

Let's forget

Let's close our eyes
forget the world
Give me sighs
And happy cries

We can run away
To the edge of town
Refuse to let it
Get us down

Let's close our eyes
forget the world
Give me sighs
And happy cries

Stop the clock
Turn off the lights
Shine our smiles
On darkest nights

Let's close our eyes
forget the world
Give me sighs
And happy cries

When we open
back up again
Let's hope
It's not all gone
insane

Let's close our eyes
forget the world
Give me sighs
And happy cries

Moments that heal

Side by side
A lazy afternoon
Piled on the bed
Socked feet tangled
Faces pressed close

Not much said
Just the laughter
And stretch of lips
Until cheeks hurt
And sides stitch

Time quickly slips
Instead of stalls
And for a moment
It's all okay again

Magic tricks

The barest touch
Of your fingers
Through my hair

So swiftly soothe
The viscous pursuit
By these hounds
Of hell

Turned to kittens
That purr
And knead
And lick rough tongues

On the back
Of my trembling hand
And the sand
Drips by the hour

And no matter
What life's planned
In that moment
It all stands still

When I close
These exhausted eyes
And salted tracks fallen
from dark skies

I cling
So desperate
To momentary highs
And whisper
Penny wishes
For more of these
Contented sighs

Making mundane beautiful

Something as little
As your hand in mine
Through the mundane

Can cause my heart
To jump
Off that steep precipice

Before it tumbles down
Kamikaze style
Back to where it all began

Momentary pauses

Pressure upon constant pressure
Between the temples
And between the lines

Built, task by task, by task
Then thought by thought
Before winched together

For each moment of every day
Where responsibility lay
Piled until it blocks out the sun

And the very idea of fun
Until for a just a moment
The only thought is of you

Love and Cheese – Shannon McEwen

Moments like this

We played
All afternoon
In brilliant rays
Of August sun

Water splashes
Bubbling flashes
Of happy laughs
Makes for silly fun

Fresh berries
And salty kisses
On warm skin
I come undone

A moment
Pressed gently
Into the pages
Of my mind

Moments of clarity

A song of angels
Soft melodies
Invoke memories

Of my eyes
Meeting yours
Just before
my fingers
So boldly cupped
wet cheeks

And whispered words
Right to your soul
Where in that moment

We made
one another
Whole

"It's all going to be ok"
Went far beyond
The words

Love and Cheese – Shannon McEwen

My love

Never half-hearted
All or nothing
From the nakedness
Of this tattered
And bruised soul

I will give
Every single thing
I am or can be
To the very last word

Not just skin deep
But slowly seep
So far in
Until I walk through
Soul to soul
Talk to you

Whisper reassurance
In dark of night
Hold your hand
Wrap all that's me
Around you

Despite wet grains
Of times sand
And when you
May lose sight
I'll hold you close

But remember
As fully as this
Fills all of your
Empty spaces
Without a reason
To keep going
Can just as quickly
Disintegrate.

My world right

I watch as you sleep
Long lashes swept across pale cheeks

A hint of a smile plays
The warmth of your hand
Laid on a hip without thought

Soft noises as with my lips
I adore you

Beautiful blue eyes flutter
Hazy with remnants of slumber
A flare of desire

Such depth within a gaze
Locked
Full of promise

And with a look
You set my world right

Moments of peace

Music bounces
Off sparkling lights
Darkest nights

Softly dimmed
By the twinkle
In your eyes

Mixed boldly with
My happy sighs
And for a moment

Life is good
Dreams carry
On all that could

And love is right
Just for once
Lights up night

Where the dark
Is briefly forgotten
And peace sparks

Music Therapy

Sitting in this shadowed room
Shrugging off this lingering gloom

Reaching out to better thoughts
Battles won, and depressions lost

Thinking of the very things
That cause my lips to lift and sing

 In a very off-key kind of way
Until darkness quietly slinks away

And I'm left only with your affection
In this shady afternoon reflection

Love and Cheese – Shannon McEwen

Near or far

In the blink of an eye
Time has flown
So swiftly by

Your hand nestled
So sweetly in mine
And still your kisses

Madly divine
Like the first touch
Of lips

That shot sparks
To the very edges
Of my fingertips

Yet even more
Than before
My love for you

Has grown more
Than I could
Have ever known

As I press you near
Or even far away
I still know

Your love
Is always
Right here

Perfect fit

Stubborn fits of unreasonable ire
Stunted episodes of fervent desire

Clashes of two such dissimilar minds
Embedded within the tie that binds

Rumour has it that opposites attract
Improbable judging by how we react

Lover's who seem to be out of groove
So much to lose and nothing to prove

One of a pair, two of a different kind
Why we have combined comes to mind

Out of sorts and constantly misunderstood
Always stuck on he should, or she could

But when I step into your arms
And briefly partake in your charms

Even I must solemnly admit
You and I are a perfect fit

Love and Cheese – Shannon McEwen

Poem to a sleeping love

Kiss me in the morning
In the subtle golden light
From the breaking of day
Until the darkest of night

Hold me right up close
Hearts pressed, beat by beat
In rhythm and constant rhyme
Sizzle as our eyes meet

Love me like you want to
Until every single fibre sings
Heart, soul, and in-between
Give me all your love brings

And never, never leave me be
From this breaking of the day
To the very uncertain end
In your life baby, I shall stay

Raindrop dreams

Fat raindrops splat
Onto my windshield

Brings me to a place
A very lovely space
Of fantastical dreams

Where salted drops fall
In freshly brilliant reams
And everything
Is exactly as it seems

Open window
With crumpled sheets
Fresh renewals aroma
Mix with rapid heartbeats

And worry
Takes a very back seat

In this imaginary bed
Where we lay our heads
So very close together
With tangled feet

Love and Cheese – Shannon McEwen

Rare moments of nothing

Where there is sweet nothing
Except the beat of our hearts
In companionable rhythm

Flesh to flesh with no rush
Just silence and stillness
Basking in this rare moment

Between the constant chaos
And ever revolving world
A space to stop and just be

Truly you combined with me
Nothing else but the feel of
The peaceful presence of us

Reasons why

Long after my bones
Have turned to dust
From this life
To the next
Then the next

The wind will speak
To my soul
Of how you
Kept me whole
Despite the storms
Regardless of fate

You remain the love
That balances the hate
And stalled the devil
From my gate

A solid foundation
Mingled with tears
crushed my fears
And holds strong
All these years

Love and Cheese – Shannon McEwen

Tick tock of hearts

Every second
Ticks by -- Like your heart beat
Next to mine
And the thought - of you
Makes me feel
Just fine
Because I know
Your words
Aren't just another line
But a promise
So utterly sublime
As to draw
An invisible visage
Here in the recesses
Of my busy mind
Where we swim
Snuggle
Walk and climb
Cry, try and sing
And laugh so hard
Our cheeks
Hurt for weeks
And love so much
In action
The words are simply
A lovely addition
To everything
You do to show me
So, I'll just close
My eyes while we're apart
Listen to the clock
To hear our hearts
And know
Our love is here inside
Where all beautiful
Things reside

Reassurances

These parched lips
Plant a seed
A soft kiss
to forehead

Hesitant fingers
Reach out
Trace path down
Wet cheeks

These green eyes
Peer so deep
Into yours

Where my soul
Whispers
Ever so softly
It'll be ok

Remind me

Let's close the curtains
Shut off the sun
Pull back the covers
And have some fun

A pillow fight
Mirth takes flight
And love replenishes
Regains its sight

Take me back to that first kiss
Lip to lip let's make a wish
To remember to pause
And sometimes rewind

Love me soundly
Before pulling tight
Breathe in this peace
That makes it right

As I drift to sleep
Look into my eyes
Keep my soul together
Mend these broken ties

Seeing you

Curve of face
You concentrate
In intimate space

Feel the right place
As you move
Without thought

Not realizing
Sweet emotions
You've wrought

As I watch you
And love you too
Even when I'm

Just a little blue
You make this love
Feel so brand new

Love and Cheese – Shannon McEwen

Snapshots of you

Romantic interludes fade
Make way
for toddler "adventures"

Leisurely hours once spent
Turn to brief glances
 In the constant passing

To somewhere else we must be
Where responsibility waits
and schedules reign

Leaving me here
 And you there
Except in cerebral image

Where we lay entwined
the clock stops ticking
And all I can see
Is you.

Soaking up the sun

I sit here
And hold dear
Memories

Between now
And that
Single moment

Where I looked
So deep
Into the beauty
That's you

Just before
your essence
soaked
Into my soul

Solid ground

Doubt the world
And doubt me too
But look deep
Into my eyes
See the love

Stop this
Pointless worry
All these imagined
Goodbyes

Remember
It's not just you
Who fears
Or cries

Tell those voices
Inside your head
To stop spilling
Hateful lies

Doubt it all
And doubt me too
Words are words
But my eyes
Don't lie

Thank you

For being my voice when I had none
Holding every piece together
When the softest wind
Made me come wholly undone

Holding my hand
Every time I faltered
Providing a reason
To ignore my reflection
In the hourglass that cracked
And bled tiny grains of sand

The words that spilled
From your love
To my brain
That hugged me tight
Before they filled

Empty crevices and space
That slowly help redraw
From mind to soul
The very image
Of this woman's face

Love and Cheese – Shannon McEwen

The best medicine

I want to bury my worries
Beneath the shadow
Created by you
Holding me

Where light
Doesn't have to be
To show radiance

I want to forget my troubles
In the space
Between your lips
And mine

Where love
Erases all else
But the vision
Of you
Holding me

And the light
That shines from your eyes
Where worries evaporate
And troubles vanish

Left with only
The love

The point of no return

Not that everything you do
Has gone unnoticed
Or unappreciated
Even unloved

But in that beautiful second When
Without hesitation
Your gentle hands
Cleaned fragrant
Regurgitated
Chunks of banana
From the interior
Of my car
I knew.

You are the man of my dreams
Come true.

Love and Cheese – Shannon McEwen

The question of romance

It's not just an answer
To a well-placed query
It's an impromptu dance

Where we get caught
Between a glance
And intimate embrace

Or when fingers
Slowly, softly
With grace
Trace every line
In my upturned face

It's a walk
With just you
And the moon
Fingers entwined

Stepping to the tune
Of our rapid beats
Where we race
To get somewhere
Then sleep 'til noon

It's a single flower
In an unusual hour
A simple note
Or a quote
Left to denote

The very core
Of our souls
And the reminder
That a piece of me
Makes you whole

Sanity within insanity

At the end of the day
When all the lights dim
And the constant chaos

Finally softens
To a dull growl
Except the love

I feel
From tip of baby toe
To the depth of my soul

I remember
The significance of you
And me

Love and Cheese – Shannon McEwen

Utopia

The yawning sun peaks
Through our Venetian blinds

Incessant sounds of traffic fade away
Along with the tick, ticking of the clock

The soft whir of the fan Breathes
Early morning air across my back

Your beautiful eyes look back
And everything is alright

When love IS the norm

Once my heartbeat slowed
And the lights turned off
The music turned to silence
And reality became the norm

Yet it remains
Between the curtains
Through darkness
And reality be damned

Because love is
In the very fabric of life
With you

Love and Cheese – Shannon McEwen

Love the most

Where your soul
Ends and mine
Begins
Bright lights
Blended lines
Blinds our eyes
And magic
Sparkles
Crackles around
Our toes
Where we step
Disoriented
Not sure
The direction
We came from
Or where we're
Headed
lighthearted
From touching
The stardust
Before it exploded
And soaked
Into our mingled souls
Where we embrace
Such beauty
Traced
The colours
Raced through
Our celestial veins
Before separating
Us back
Into our bones
Hand in hand
Leaving us here
Not quite sure
Of where we were

Running amok

My love runs out
To the very tips
Of your almost
Perfect lips

Pink tongue
That flicks
As laughter
Fills my lungs

My love runs out
To slowly wrap
Sensuously around
Every curve

And clings
To that sound
You make when
You're happy

My love runs out
Into a sappy
Little pile
And goes
For miles
    And miles
        And miles
And never meets
The very end

Day of rest

Lazy Sunday morning
Where it's hard to tell
Where you end
I begin

Tangled limbs
Layered in answered whims
Mingled with happy grins

Green eyes mesh
With deeper blue
Back to green

Deeper meaning
Between me
And you

Every wish received
Happiness believed

In the bright light of day
Nothing left to say
Every needed word said
And inner fear laid dead

As we lay here
Limbs tangled
And Love fed

Stargazing

A sky spattered
With brightest stars
Sitting here
Just where we are

Warmth embraces
Our stargazing eyes
Muffled by
Our satiated sighs

And the universe smiles
Because you
And me
We're meant to be

Love and Cheese – Shannon McEwen

Sweetest dreams

I'm in my dreaming tree
Thinkin' about me
Tangled up with you

In this steamy place
Where time ain't ticking
And no tock either

Just this fever
Takin' up plenty of space
Making hearts race

And profound tears
Trickling down
My upturned face

So here I sit
Within my mind
Pressing against the glass

Seeing beauty
In every sight I see
Starting with you
Then adding me

Thoughts of you

Clenching, fluttering
Beating intensified
Boiling
My heart at
The thought of you

Tingling, warming
Goose fleshed
Alive
My skin at
The thought of you

Swirling, filling
Lighting the darkness
Reeling
My Mind at
The thought of you

Stopping, electrifying
Ragged intake
Slow exhale
My breath at
The thought of you

Flying, Soaring
Singing in tune
Whole
My soul at
The thought of you

Tropical wishes

White fabric
Flicks
   Undulates
Dances with
  Tropical breeze

Softly brushes
  Across sheets
To caress
    Warm skin

Nestled within
    white cotton
Two lovers
   Limbs Entwined
Pause button
  Ready to press
Rewind

To replay it
All over again
   In a dream
Reams
     And reams
Of warm sighs
  Fevered cries

And the wish
  To stay within
This amazing place
Warm and loved
  In this incredible
Space

What you do to me

When your eyes meet mine
Across a crowded room
My heart skips a beat
The flesh of my body tingles
As lips curve in response
To the incredible lightness
Of limb and heart
That explodes
Through every vein

When your gaze locks mine
I melt
A pool of liquid
As my pulse races
My eyes trace your face
A sigh escapes
Unable to turn away
The connection felt
To my soul

Love and Cheese – Shannon McEwen

What he thinks

His eyes crinkle
At the edges
As he contemplates
How someone
In a wheelchair
would get by
The construction signs
Haphazardly
Placed across the sidewalk
And his frown
Soft voice turned down
As he talks
And my love abounds
Here In the interior
Of this van
For this man
Who always thinks
of such things

Through the lens

She captures
The beauty you dare
Not see

Because then you'd
Have no reason
To be
Disappointed

Between the fantasy
Of what life
Should be
And the reality

That imperfections
Demonstrate

Inspections
Of faith
Demand
Truth not be blind

Yet be kind
But your amazing eyes
Swim in tears

From these years
Of self propelled
Reflection
Of every flaw
And every sin

Always focused
So deep within
Whilst grace
abounds

Love and Cheese – Shannon McEwen

When the same eyes
Hear my similar sighs

And such love
Resounds
Here in my heart
At this image I see
Of you in my lens

Of not what you can be
Or change
Or do or see
But here and now

In the lines of jaw
Long lashes that surround
Depths of blue
And endless hues
Of all the chaos
That is wholly, beautifully
You

The wonder of you

When you say just the right words
That I need to hear
The world all around us
Crumbles away and disappears

And all that's left
Is the sound of your beating heart
In rhythm with mine
And despite the chaos
Outside this space
Or inside my mind
I know innately
That it's gonna be just fine
That all I must do
Is to wrap these arms around you
And hold on tight

Because in this this crazy life
We may lose sight
Of what is right
Here in what goes wrong
In all the shiny lights
And nightmare filled nights
Or never-ending, task filled throng
Of expectations
To do's, reports, meetings
Repeating's
When you say just the right words
That I need to hear
The world all around us
Crumbles away and disappears

And all that's left
Is the sound of your beating heart
In rhythm with mine
And despite the chaos

Love and Cheese – Shannon McEwen

Outside this space
Or inside my mind
I know innately
That it's gonna be just fine

When I sink to my knees
At the end of my rope
And I think
I can't take another step
you look into these eyes
And without a blink
You link your fingers with mine
And tell me you wouldn't lie
That if it weren't for me
You couldn't get by

That you and I
are made of hope
and faith and love
and those beautiful blue eyes
look so deeply into these green
bring such wonder
I've never seen

That only divine things
Could have brought this love
Into being
When you say just the right words
That I need to hear
The world all around us
Crumbles away and disappears

And all that's left
Is the sound of your beating heart
In rhythm with mine
And despite the chaos
Outside this space
Or inside my mind I know innately
That it's gonna be just fine

For the love of brussel sprouts

You smile and say
Brussel sprouts
Don't tell a story
Of love

I just laugh
And accept that
Cookies and tea
Maybe a lovely scene
But with a twinkle
And grin

And uplifted chin
I prove you a little wrong
Because although
These little green balls
May have a bad rep

Boiled
Into every little kids
Christmas dinner nightmares
One things for sure

Every year without compare
Those little cabbages
Show up
Stout tradition
On the Christmas rendition

Year in
Year out
Dependable
Defendable
To the bitter end
My little friends are always there

Love and Cheese – Shannon McEwen

Never fail
When I need them
Never changing
Ever raging
Inside my stomach

Passionately reminding me
Of the festivities
I've just partaken
Never forsaken me

So, my dearest love
Brussel sprouts
Can and do represent
Our current love

You just must think
Outside what
Your Romantic heart
Was trying
To think of

A billion plus one

How much do I love you?
My love
A billion plus one
Plus some
What's in the plus?
A peanut butter
And pickle sandwich
Some advice
That turned out
Half right
And a million kisses
Across lips
To say goodnight
Where we lay
On a blanket
Side by side
Hands held tight
Looking at the moon
And the stars
And singing along
With the fork and the spoon
About coming home soon
To you

Love and Cheese – Shannon McEwen

Sharing the wonder

Scenery flashes by
Almost
As fast

My mind sees
Little bits
Of wonder

In the sunshine
Green of trees
Or branches laid bare

Myriad of traffic
Rushing somewhere
Between
Here and there

And I sigh
Because I want
To share it all
with you

So, I'm trying to capture
Every little detail
So you can feel
The wonder too

Held

Jesus took our hands
And he placed them
Into each other's

And then placed
His own on top
And his ethereal
Eyes
Shone into mine

And his beautiful voice
Echoed
So deeply into my heart

As he said
These words that poured
Into me
Filling every empty space
Tears dripping
Down this upturned face

I give you him
And him you
To love each other
Him to teach you
How to love me
Like he loves me so deep

And you to teach him
How to love himself
How you will love him
In the same way

Without boundaries
Conditions or fear

Love and Cheese – Shannon McEwen

And then he simply
Held us near
His teardrop mingled
With ours

His sacrifice
So great
It washed us clean

And suddenly
I knew
It didn't matter
What others thought

It only mattered
What I knew
Right here
Deep in my heart

About the Author

Shannon McEwen has been a poet from the age of five, finding inspiration in every aspect of her life, from her experiences, emotions and the people with whom she interacts. She sees beauty everywhere and is acutely in tune with the energy and emotions of people in her life and even some who just cross her path.

Poetry is a passion for Shannon, and as natural and required as breathing. She leaves an infinitesimal piece of her soul in every word that she strings together.

In her Professional life, Shannon is a people leader with a passion for building teams. She lives in Surrey with her gorgeous kids, who of course, are her greatest inspirations of all. Although her Fiancé is a close second for inspiration, considering he at times turns her poetry into lyrics and sings them to her and is a talented poet/songwriter in his one right.

This is Shannon's second book, her first, Cracks in my Soul, A journey between Darkness and light, was also published by Filidh Publishing.

Love and Cheese – Shannon McEwen